PILOTS AND NAVIGATORS

for Sally,

thanks for having me

xox

Pilots and Navigators

ANTONY DUNN

Oxford   New York
OXFORD UNIVERSITY PRESS
1998

Oxford University Press, Great Clarendon Street, Oxford OX2 6DP

Oxford New York

Athens Auckland Bangkok Bogotá Buenos Aires Calcutta
Cape Town Chennai Dar es Salaam Delhi Florence Hong Kong Istanbul
Karachi Kuala Lumpur Madrid Melbourne Mexico City Mumbai
Nairobi Paris São Paulo Singapore Taipei Tokyo Toronto Warsaw
and associated companies in Berlin Ibadan

Oxford is a registered trade mark of Oxford University Press

© Antony Dunn 1998

The moral rights of the author have been asserted

First published in Oxford Poets
as an Oxford University Press paperback 1998

British Library Cataloguing in Publication Data
Data available

Library of Congress Cataloging in Publication Data
Dunn, Antony, 1973–
Pilots and navigators / Antony Dunn.
(Oxford poets)
I. Title. II. Series
PR6054.U535P55 1998   821'.914—dc21   98–3209
ISBN 0–19–288095–0

10 9 8 7 6 5 4 3 2 1

Typeset by George Hammond Design
Printed in Great Britain by Athenæum Press Ltd.
Gateshead, Tyne and Wear

ACKNOWLEDGEMENTS

are due to the editors of the following publications:
Artbeat, The Independent, Lines Review, The Month, The New Welsh Review, Oxford Poetry, Oxford Quarterly Review, Phoenix, Quartos, The Reader, Remolo.

Four poems were published in the Varsity/Cherwell May Anthologies of 1994 and 1995, edited by Bernard O'Donoghue and Ted Hughes respectively. Several were broadcast by BBC Radio York in August and November 1997. 'Bardney Woods' won first prize in the 1992 Yorkshire Open Poetry Competition, 'Judith with the Head of Holofernes' was the winner of the Sir Roger Newdigate Prize in 1995, and 'Lisdoonvarna' was a major prize-winner in the 1997 Cardiff International Poetry Competition.

I owe a particular debt to Paul Burbridge, Nigel Forde, David Hughes, Peter James and Bernard O'Donoghue for their tireless help and encouragement.

for Vicki

'*Two things are happening at once, one telling me I am where I am, the other cutting me loose.*'

Andrew Motion, *Sailing To Italy*

CONTENTS

Bardney Woods   1
Biology Lesson   2
Young Ornithologist   3
Downhill   4
Bournemouth   5
Drifting Off   6
Plymouth to Exeter   9
Drive   10
Something to Say   11
Blackpool   12
Up the Chevin   13
Waltz   14
Underground   15
Vicki Watches the Perseids   16
Tadpoles   17
Voyage without Instruments   18
Hull to Brugge   19
Dublin   20
Lisdoonvarna   24
Robinson Meets Prytherch   26
From Wrexham   27
Origami   28
Narnia   29
Robinson to his Neighbour in the Dole Queue   30
Branwell among his Sisters   31
Judith with the Head of Holofernes   32
What We Remember   33
Storm Warning   34
Kiss   35
Cooking for One   37
You   38
Halloween   39
From Portmeirion   40

From Snowdon   41
In the Time it Takes   42
Orchard   43
Engagement   44
Apology   46
Proposal   47
White Dress   48
Dummy   49
His and Hers   50
Cocoon   51
Sunday Ordinariness   52
Cockatoo   53
Secret Marriage   54
Toast   55
Last Train Home   55

BARDNEY WOODS

Cycling through the trees we burst
out on to bumpy concrete.

This is where the Dambusters
took off from. Spokes mangle air

as we stand on pedals and
heave our machines into life.

Elbows are wings and the wind
is pretend engines as we

lumber along the runway
like the ghosts of Lancasters.

A tug at the handlebars
and the front wheel leaves the ground

for a breathless moment, then
back to earth with a wobble.

Lapwings, startled from the grass,
flick skywards in eye-corners

and, as we skid to a stop
where concrete runs out beneath

our wheels, fly towards the sun,
touching us with their shadows.

BIOLOGY LESSON

When we were fourteen we planted
beans in jars, squeezed between the glass
and the damp pink blotting paper.

We also scooped frog spawn from ponds,
and kept that behind glass as well.
We did not understand, then, why

after such a rush of good shoots,
such prodigious sprouting of legs,
the leaves died yellow and tiny
and no frog stepped on to the stone.

Of this class of fourteen–year olds—
the females introduced this year—
we can expect a good number
to blossom quickly; healthily.

YOUNG ORNITHOLOGIST

The names of those places have slipped away,
and I doubt I could tell a siskin from
a greenfinch these days, certainly not by
their songs alone.

The prime sites of Lincolnshire, Humberside,
were wide, wind-shifted estuary coasts
where the sandy grasses had been sharpened
to rustling blades

in the untrustable landscape of dunes.
But the clueless seal pup comes back sometimes;
how it lay still on the grey, open miles
of sea-inched mud

as if loneliness were all it possessed.
My one photograph captures it wrongly,
fills its space with seal, steals the moment's soul,
misremembers.

There's nothing to prove that I was lonely,
but should I ever be alone again
among sharp grasses, I might feel something
like memory,

something like a single sourceless birdsong
I almost recognize, floating in, out,
like flotsam which might have beached before, or
never before.

DOWNHILL

for Nicholas

The first I know of it is my father
locking our bikes in the shed; then he says
our uncle has died beneath a lorry
in a New York rush hour.

My brother and I, next day, steal the key
and unimpound our machines. We drag them
to the top of the hill-road, forgetful,
and trust our free descent,

coasting through the hot traffic of grasses,
pollen fumes, dodging fenders of tight bends
as if you were racing ahead into
perpetual motion

BOURNEMOUTH

The full moon on the water is a drive-in movie
no one watches. The steam-windowed car bobs as if afloat;
on the pier the four-legged, four-armed, two-headed freakshow
kneads its own breasts and begs itself to stop, harder, stop;
six kids in a metro, skinning up, wild with the munchies;
a pensioner, slow-eyed, ashy reefer poised at the down-wound
    glass;
the pinafored waitress, staring out, absently touching herself
in the lighted first-floor window of an empty fish restaurant;
and we, four actors, silhouette ourselves on the screen of the sky,
obnoxious as a fat toe-trampler in a cramped cinema.

The audience, familiar as stereotypes,
as troubled by our passing as the sea by a skimmed stone,
ignores the unreeled sand where its own, its true story
is played out quietly by a cast of dumb extras.
Two fishermen cyclopsed in miner's helmets catch nothing
while a monochrome drunk balances on the water's edge,
    miming
a shouting above the din of the surf into his mobile phone.
Suddenly he is dead still, legs apart, canute-small, phone held
    high
as if the argument of the ocean might explain everything
to whoever it is that cannot listen to him speaking.

DRIFTING OFF

Home after seven months on tour, I walk
across the village green to the low bridge.
After all these years I still haven't found
where this water comes from, or to which stretch
of sea it abandons its sheepish course.
Through new-grass-scented dark, along the stream,
sidles the somewhere smell of Camden Lock,
as if budding broom and bridal bouquet
were so many hot-dog stands, new-age stalls,
cherry blossom the slicks of Thames traffic.

* * *

I don't remember punting anyone
nowhere and back through green Isis willows.

* * *

That night, when we climbed the fence of the University Parks,
keel-hammered a bin for a cargo of anglo-saxon notes
and balanced it on the blackened Cherwell, then set it alight,
a mirrored fire turned slowly out of reach. We might have seen it
burning still miles away, but it was hidden by that midnight's
countless invisible banks and branches; then onset of day.

* * *

I never once made a tuxedoed dive
from Magdalen Bridge in the May Morning dawn.

* * *

And then that time Tony bought cockles from the indoor market
and poured them from the bridge, shouting, *swim back to the sea,*
    be free;
when we laughed as if we had not been too squeamish to take
    home
the puffy and flaccid baby octopi from the deli,
as if there were not precedent enough for the dead being
sent to the ocean and whatever valhalla lies beyond.

* * *

Why do we choose riverbanks for endings?
The choking sandwiches in the parked car
and the dumb staring at the thick water,
the stupid, relentless, urgent water.

* * *

And yet what I'm trying to talk about
is the speeding apart of things, watching
a water that will converge and converge
with water upon water to become
one water, one determined aimless surge;

when what I mean is more the every star
rushing away from every star, quiet
in its immeasurable haste. But this
failed gravity is not enough, which leaves
our charts honest for fleet thousands of years.

* * *

And I never shared a sleeping bag
on a roof awash with starlight and empties.

* * *

7

Tonight will be our last chance to watch the aimless
two thousand year comet, coming, going;
and it's cloudy. I suffer vertigo, staring
upwards, as if down from night's chalky edge.

An occasional star needles the wheeling dark,
the wind scratching through branches like the sound
of the last groove of your favourite LP in that
stretched second before the stylus lifts off.

* * *

What brings all this to mind is the lone drive
in the tour van across the Tamar bridge;
as the stars crystallize, as the question
of who I am clears into where I am
going. And to the toll-man I am two
fleet tail-lights, then part of the sudden dark.

PLYMOUTH TO EXETER

Halfway from naval base to north-bound motorway
the three of you were sleepers in a nest of books,
scraps of scrabble scores, earphones, mineral waters,
as the crash barrier ahead unfolded wings
and launched a grey heron into watery air.

Porpoising seriously alongside the van,
three feet from wing-tip to wing-mirror, it kept up
for ten seconds, or twenty, insisting *this way*
as if there were no other way, as if there were
something beneath the surface of things to steer round.

I might have woken you, but the invisible
reef was like a loss, a homesickness too soon.
Arrowing an unreadable chart *you are here*
the heron held, held, then tacked up, behind, tidy
as a heap of clothes folded on an empty beach.

DRIVE

In the road-movie dust and crunch of dry ground
I step from the van into the baked lay-by.
Parked on a hill, watching your parents' village
where you sometimes live, I could almost miss you.

I stay too long. Desperate. My piss curves out
like gold-spun straw, and runs and evaporates
over the breeze-blurred tracks. The warm, solid earth
wants nothing to do with my passing presence.

You are thirty miles away. Impermeable.
I salute your house, dry-mouthed; unnoticed, start
the engine as if there were twenty cop cars
in the rear-view and a canyon's edge ahead.

SOMETHING TO SAY

Across the shrugging Pennines, with the sky
mad orange and pink ahead,
the mirrors deepening to an unlikely blue,

we were drinking curious green cola,
struggling not to tell our truths,
when one song from the bland cassette stalled my pulse.

Wishing our van would wing up and after
the ridiculous sunset,
I held fast to the dangerous wheel, listening.

BLACKPOOL

for Vicki, Louise & Paul

I've been watching the curtains
of the rooms where you are sleeping.
Two hours in the early sun
of the nine-month tour's final day,
waiting for words for this calm,
this stillness of the poised instant
at the top of the highest
roller-coaster in the country,
when inexorable rails
drop, swerve invisibly away,
the brief horizontalling
of untrustworthy horizons.

I've been watching the curtains,
stomach and heart mashed in clenched hold,
waiting for the unseen lurch
of eyelids, the stretched foot from sheets
that will push this hanging world
into its long, sick, tilted rush.
I would keep you here, all three,
boil water for coffee, toast bread,
lay tables, open curtains
in this stranger's home, miles from homes.
And yet. The curtains. Wake up,
there's so much I want to tell you.

UP THE CHEVIN

From the rock this view of our shoes
a hundred feet above the ground,
of sodium lights along the road
away from Leeds into the hills,
of each tree becoming part of forest
under the sharpening moon,

as if everything were remembering itself
for a moment in the blurring dusk—
as if two things were happening at once.

WALTZ

Around the library, port glasses,
emptied or abandoned, are printing
party diagrams on to smart wood.

One expert couple is still dancing
as the band slows into a last waltz
and you pull me to my clumsy feet.

Neither of us can dance. Like strangers,
my arm round the warm violin-curve
of your waist, the slack bow of your hair

across my nervous lips and taut neck,
we scuff each other's shoes, unsure who's
leading whom around the turning room.

We are lost beneath these tall windows,
stumbling heart of the astrolabe night,
discovering who we are, and where.

UNDERGROUND

Hard to be sympathetic through the crush
of escalators to another platform
when some miserable jumper has shocked
the Central line to a breathless stop.

Forgive me if I press your head too hard
to my chest as we sway round the Circle,
feeling for the vibrations of your blood,
the heart's traffic roaring through unmapped veins,

for the regular pulse of air rushed out
ahead of something about to arrive.

VICKI WATCHES THE PERSEIDS

We anticipate them for so long
that they are a shock when they come

roaring quietly across vast
millimetres of eye-corner dark.

We can't be sure what is seen, what dreamt.
Something tears between us—a breath

which might have been *I love you*—sure as
a quick light's ghost on the retina.

TADPOLES

Evolution in a plastic bucket.
Silly spawn leaps from species to species
quicker than a spring term.

Now your plastic gifts. How you teach me that
we can't run before we can breathe raw air.
Limb by lung, quietly.

VOYAGE WITHOUT INSTRUMENTS

Legend has it that my great-grandfather arrived
in England by boat,
rowed solo across the Baltic Sea to escape.

No doubt there were his secret Scyllas and Sirens
with which to contend,
a Circe to confiscate compass and sextant,

but his unerring navigational guesswork—
turn your back and heave—
(which is the only evidence of my descent)

brought him to a wife he didn't yet recognize,
who couldn't make out
his strange tongue, his having been away for ever.

No charts or logs, trunked in attics, exist as proof:
something in the blood,
merely, the way I prow a beach, watching the wake.

HULL TO BRUGGE

Fourteen hours on the overnight ferry.
A frozen, day-long slog through mapped Brugge.

Chocolate, lace, the fabled phial of Christ's blood
wombed in the garish gold basilica,

the empty square where we snap each other
plugging the mermaid statue's spouting breasts,

and then we share a room for the first time.
Coyly pyjama'd, in bunks which slide us

imperceptibly sideways back to Hull,
we turn in the tight dark and engine-pulse.

In the next cabin our friend wakes up sick—
the ocean calm as a stilled Galilee—

as her secret stowaway finds itself
casting off, pioneering a voyage

which none of us can remember making,
which none of us will know about for weeks,

but which makes this berthing in Humber dawn
a new found land, a country to explore.

DUBLIN

I

Only rain hazes the quivering air
where the moon combs Holyhead's horizon,
lifts pretty silhouettes to its bright eye
then drops them back into grainy darkness.

Stirring this wet sky, black-foamed Irish Sea,
we steal from Wales under cover of night
and are chased into Ireland by the dawn
which is waiting, not breathless, when we dock.

We have taken low stars for Dublin's lights,
low clouds for mountains beyond Dun Laoghaire,
and vice versas for both mistakes. There's mist
where the unfathomable sky begins.

II

Where the unfathomable sky begins
begins land that is nothing emerald,
save between the facets of Phoenix Park,
which is flawed by concrete and penguin muck.

No one knows the west better than our map
but here it's forgetful in smaller streets.
Oisin would have pitied our restless feet,
would not have trusted to this foreign guide.

We lose a morning to closed museums
and then ditch the map on Yeats's doorstep.
Drink in the first open pub, be aimless,
look only at things that are in your way.

III

Look only at things that are in your way,
do not encourage beggars by giving,
a guidebook's an invite to a mugging,
two eggs for boys, cruet-duty for girls:

our landlady's constant as the Liffey.
She knows a town from thirty years ago
and says she has no personal callers,
but there is a Jesus in every room.

Thousands have broken fast at her table
and yet she's come to know not one of them.
Pounds and pence to her, unmysterious,
we will leave as if we had never been.

IV

We will leave as if we had never been
to this island unexotic as home.
No tan, no souvenirs, but we have drunk
Guinness within sight of its silver spring.

We do not cross a visible border
as the ferry hauls out Irish waters
from beneath its keel. Welsh sea looks the same.
We stand guessing Holyhead out of mist.

One harbour heaves towards us, one away,
stacked with their same freight-trucks; a short crossing,
waved-off, met, by cranes in two grey docks where
only rain hazes the quivering air.

LISDOONVARNA

1931

As if the sea had gathered itself up
and heaved its solid mass on to the sand,
a blue whale, helpless in its own tonnage,
drying on the strand near Lisdoonvarna.

The boy was five when he crested the dune
and faced the mountain head, the eyes as big
as motor lamps, when his twin sister hid
behind him saying, *save me from it, John*.

Stricken U-boat, sick kraken; a marvel
before which he held his forgotten net
like a trident, powerful as a god,
a tiny Poseidon touching the beast

until the men came, and shouted for wood
and buckets, and slung a catamaran
beneath the patient hulk, while the women
and children watered the steaming shoulders.

Well, they floated it alright, and went off
to the craic and fire of the village pub,
and the boy heard their singing from the beach
as he watched the whale, helpless as a wave,

turn about and climb back on to the sand,
huffing and whistling into its death-place
and fixing with one eye the lonely boy
standing up to his waist in the water

flinging handfuls of sea at its great head
and shouting *breathe, now, breathe* in his right air.

ROBINSON MEETS PRYTHERCH

Ordering the same beer in a Welsh pub;
Prytherch in Welsh, Robinson
in that Pennine English which
betrays his Frisco heritage; elbows

bump over the damp bar and beer is spilt.
Nothing is said, but the two
retreat to their opposite
corners, glowering their hostilities.

Robinson covets the sour old bastard's
proximity to the fire,
Prytherch the ignorant yank's
distance from the new juke-box; and Tom Jones

harps on about the *green green grass of home*
as the two sit like summit
delegates, and stubbornly
refuse either chairman or translator.

FROM WREXHAM

You came out of Wales an Englishwoman
and only the adoption papers explain
your lust for the Welsh hills,
the way you smooth your tongue
around your own language
which you pronounce perfectly
but which you cannot understand.

On the other hand, let me suggest this
in a language which we might all comprehend:
what are our borders but
adoption papers for
homelands born of no one?
You do not romanticize,
can see Welsh hills from Chester.

ORIGAMI

The Japanese cure for any sickness
is to flock the sick-bed with paper cranes.

He is taught by a girl, half Japanese,
to crease into the box-nest of white sheets

the countless improbable triangles.
This making three dimensions out of two

seems as magic as any medicine,
and the touch of fingers along each fold

is the building of something from nothing.
His first solo attempts are not tidy,

but he litters his bed with paper cranes,
their foreign superstitions facing east

to the white hospital where she will learn
the science and the maths of medicine,

as if they might take flight after her flight,
or ease his new unfamiliar pangs.

NARNIA

Not snow but mud, and deciduous trees
surround the green, ordinary lamp post
which we cannot make rightly fantastic.
Odd to be standing here, the two of us,
entire populace of this tiny world
of light, scooped out of its own universe
and placed, wrongly, back. We are nowhere new.
Without our imaginings we travel
into a real and undamaged darkness
and, tearing our jeans on witchy brambles,
we push through black, invisible branches,
finding no wardrobe door and no way out.

ROBINSON TO HIS NEIGHBOUR
IN THE DOLE QUEUE

Only days after I had blacked the eye
of a cruel friend who exposed my card trick
in the playground,
I guessed at the magician's sleight of hand
and was hushed by the birthday boy's mother.

There's something suspicious about a man
who can shred tissue paper and unfold
the sheet intact,
but cannot restore the two fingers which
the Germans magicked away years before.

We learn not to be fooled by tooth fairies
or the Budget, and choose new illusions.
All we hope for
is to put our finger on the right cup
once in a while, to turn anything up.

BRANWELL AMONG HIS SISTERS

Something to do with a failure to master oils
is bringing Branwell, year by year,
out of his own painting; the classical column
between Charlotte and Emily
giving up the ghost of its modest creator.
What self-hate haunts this painting-out,
or what deference to sisterhood or to space
in the composition, what lack
of mastery over human anatomy?
Stroke upon stroke—negligently
deliberate as his own obliteration
by drink and chemicals—fading,
gradual as forgiveness, fix him spirited
half away.
            Or his half-return
is chronicled here, as if he might be saying
that, having been through the *summoned
from sleep by death* thing, he has only now chosen
to take some kind of rightful place.

JUDITH WITH THE HEAD
OF HOLOFERNES

Judith cannot wait for the invention
of the camera. Posing for the umpteenth
sculpture this week, the chinking of chisels
bringing on a migraine, and that red paint
in the carpet nagging at her tired eye,
she is fast losing her fabled patience.

Besides, she feels daft standing for sculptors
and painters with her ammunition pouch
of lipstick, perfume and blade in one hand
and a big pineapple in the other—
the head of Holofernes is stinking
on a stake above the city's proud walls

while the whole paparazzi of artists
drools shamelessly over flesh, quick and dead.
The papers *will* insist on calling her
the Black Widow, and their readers, of course,
don't want to hear that God has been involved—
always sure to spoil the human angle.

Hard to look triumphant when her triumph
is so misunderstood. Best to daydream,
not interpreting pictures of herself
chained to railings, or throwing her body
beneath Nebuchadnezzar's horse. Patience.
Give them breasts and thighs for now. God later.

WHAT WE REMEMBER

What we saw of the attack was not
the petrol libation
or the offered matches,

nor the astonishment in his eyes,
nor the two fire-raisers
in the lock-up that night,

but his flight, trailing fiery wings,
over the tented lawn
outside the vicarage,

like some premonitory angel
bursting from our playground's
wreckage of burnt-out cars.

At least, this is what we recreate
of the night we were carried,
sleeping, from our thin canvas

when our mother heard screaming outside.
Three bombs have since exploded
in places I have just left,

the narrowness of my escapes
as fluid as fabled fish
which never yet took offered bait.

STORM WARNING

Frogs still execute
their legendary
weather map, gathered
in the road, waiting
for definite rain.

And they re-invent
the car as its own
distant ancestor:
half a mile from home,
just as the rain comes,

I'm out in front, two
miles per hour, flapping
my hand like a red
flag and scooping frogs
from newfangled death.

KISS

I

To explore new contours of teeth and lips,
the discovery of the tongue, like
a secret spring among rocks; this is the first
sketch of an unimaginable map.

II

Still awake as the sun stretched over the hills
to marmalade the wolds around us
we picked up our unread books
and ceased to be wheat-chameleons.
Along the greening grass we watched dawn scrubbing
night-grime from your white house, and talked
about nothing while our mouths
clamoured for toast and lip-balm.

III

Two tongues, milkshake-cool, closed in one mouth,
crushed juice from imagined strawberries.
Since that moment soft ghosts of fruit
have stalked this their dark familiar house.

IV

This kiss, the last of a multitude
which would have over-starred the universe,
is not bitter, not cold, but closed against ghosts.
Strict as the kiss of your sister's French landlady.
No Hollywood goodbye.

V

To explore new contours with an old map,
to discover only unfamiliar
fruit; this is the unimaginable
panic of homesickness. Of being lost.

COOKING FOR ONE

The unusual care with the bright knife,
silvering a cascade of rings from an onion,
halving a pepper and scooping out seeds,
hearting an avocado cautiously;
the cookery-book tidiness of bowls and pans
heaped with the diced, the chopped, the sliced, the pared.

The curt hiss of the blade through skins and cores,
and the fierce weeping which can be explained away.

The skin-scent which takes a moment to place,
waking up, of garlic harsh as love on your hands.

YOU

In a way we were looking for you then,
tramping the Cowley Road after midnight
down to the high street observatory,
the punting dock or music faculty.

Tilting up brassy bottled beers as if
to fanfare an imminent arrival
or to loud-hail some last errant boater,
then scope the sky through our thick-lensed empties.

He once said he'd like to see the future—
to measure my promised You against the fact.
That night I broke a tooth capping his beer.
He had often warned me I would do that.

HALLOWEEN

We buy a pumpkin, a box of candles.
Hands sticky from hollowing and cutting,
we wait for midnight, walk to the graveyard.
Once the seeded swell of flesh is shouldered
by a stone cross, we exchange ghost stories
in the orange safety of its wide grin.

The moon swings a steady hula, big enough,
I think, to quoit the whole of the city.
I have never seen it do this before.
As we pass wine between us, the bottle's
mouth surprises itself with quick moonlight—
an imitation as helpless as tides.

We are in our early twenties, and this
is a night for games, stalking each other
through the darknesses of tall stones and grass.
It is easy to ascribe our madness
to the moon—the surge and ebb of kisses,
the skin's hunger for unbearable cold—

but ours is not a werewolf mind. It's just
that, sometimes, we surprise ourselves like this,
so we blame gods, astrologies, toxins.
Beyond our fleshy light all is haunted:
by the fragments this bottle will become,
damped-out candle-ends, by ourselves, grown up.

We are most afraid of the future's ghosts—
of being helpless. Of the moon turning
its profile, of the fruit going to seed.
Lying still, we watch the stars pretending
that we are their immutable centre.
We try to imagine ourselves at home.

FROM PORTMEIRION

More marvellous by a stretch
is the mile of rhododendrons which pastel
the avenue out.
The italianate village
hunkers down among trees in the wing mirrors
in gradual dusk.

Out of season, the grey sea
is pacing alone the dull, unlikely sands
from where we have climbed,
as if waiting for the night—
the dark that will rob balustrades and towers
of their pale appeal—

to give it a fair excuse
to slope off on its own and to do nothing.
Pretty, we agree,
pointless; and we pull away.
And I'm watching the retraction of the last
nodding minaret

in the mirror, wondering
if it's okay to swivel the rear-view glass
to catch your eye as
the blurring rhododendrons
seem endless ahead and I hope that we reach
no way out of them.

I swing the glass, and worry
that objects in the rear-view mirror appear
closer than they are.

FROM SNOWDON

If I look at you from the west
you are against the clearest sky
and everything behind you is sharp
in the mountains' tidy air;

from the east you are turned away,
and all the sky ahead is cloud,
deep grey where sometimes we might see
ocean, another country's hills.

Just like you to stare into the invisible
while tourists steal pieces of their costly view,

to flex your mind into the measureless grey—
a gull trawling the tang of distant salt.

From where we stand, half of what we know
is the brightness behind, half the blindness ahead.
I love that you turn towards the mystery,
and how your skin dampens within the cloud;

the way you tread where the mountain
might open up before you a path
or footless ravine, and that either
is better than a bought way down.

IN THE TIME IT TAKES

Snow doubles the black apple branches
and in the early hours' orchard-light
I re-imagine myself. In smoke
clingy and faint as a drowning twin

crawling, face up, along the ceiling
of a frozen river, there I am.
I am my own shadow, an ice gap
for my opposite to not come through.

In my sheltering hand the small light,
slow fuse of a cigarette, whose charge
is either one quiet ounce of dark
or the packed and primed case of my skull.

ORCHARD

Before dawn, through cidery mist
to see the shy ruins at sunrise,
in April cold we plother and slide;
make the bold exchanges
of awake-all-night strangers,
speaking slights of breath
like verses into the branches
for no one to discover.

ENGAGEMENT

You tell me too late at night,
when all I can think of is

the clock on the kitchen wall,
hauling me towards breakfast,

bus and office. So nervous
even your grins shake, the two

of you accept the one-way
surprise of handshakes, kisses,

congratulations and tears
with patience vulnerable

to the hearty attrition
of a private joy shared out.

And no champagne in the house.
Only a bottle-bottom's

moat of wine left from dinner,
passed from lip to lip around

the kitchen table in one
glass: a communion of

differences. Mute witnesses—
garlic jar, aga, five eggs

in a bowl—absorb the news
and softly alter beyond

recovery; and sleep is
an anti-climax somehow.

*　*　*

Your kitchen might feel safe, but I tell you
this much; in the silence

between talk and laughter or whatever,
there is a noise outside.

Just as flames will not illuminate wolves
whose voices savage

the camper roomed by fire's limits, so this light
won't reveal ghosts who howl

under the door. Do you even hear them?
The boy who hanged himself

in a tree between house and village,
the biker buried by

his own machine in the dyke which, but for
the hedge, you could spit into

from the kitchen window, the tyred cats
and rabbits and the rest,

all warn you about leaving this domestic
Eden; stepping out

from the known into a world where gin-traps
and shotguns and hounds are less

ruthless than nature. Do you not hear them
at all? I hope you don't.

Do not be surprised if I raise my voice
at the strangest moments.

APOLOGY

You must forgive me when I sound as if
I am not celebrating hard enough.

Of course I am happy—there could have been
no conclusion for which I would have tossed

my top hat higher—but this happiness
is a caught bouquet. When you jointly knife

the cake you'll know what I am wishing for.
I wish you all the joy you can bear, but

some of the same for myself. All guests will
raise this quiet toast of envy: you will

be briefly perfect, and such a moment,
for us, is either far off or far gone.

PROPOSAL

It came without fuss on a motorway
in a treacherous, exciting rain-storm:
one treading the gas lightly as ballet,
one with frozen left arm, numbing to warm,

puppeteering broken windscreen wipers
with strings from the soaking passenger seat.
Tortoising the inside lane, cloud-snipers
popping at the glass, hared into retreat

by the swish and brag of a speeding Jag,
you team up; pilot and navigator.
This is no race, there is no chequered flag,
but you cross some real line a thought later,

passing the stopped show-off copulating
with crash-barriers on the verdant bank.
Visibility poor, and you, waiting
to feel you've left the place your mirror shrank

to the grey frame you're crawling away from,
peer together down the veiled road ahead,
guessing what bright towns you might light upon;
what home, what concord, what peace and what dread.

WHITE DRESS

If you insist on showing me the dress
dummied in the frothy window,
you are asking me (if you *must* ask me
how it will look) to picture you

lingeried, struggling in for the first time,
and to dream myself attendant
with the excuse of buttons or a zip
for my fastening hands at your spine.

DUMMY

It does not understand breathing space;
it has no lungs to heave against
the steel ribs of its bodice.

It is your stunt double, patiently
wearing a voodoo of pins and
the chill of unfinished work.

Its wooden foot paddles confetti
made of trimmings, buttons and
threads,
but it is as lifeless as

old photographs of the wedding of
someone you never knew. The dress
waits for more than a seamstress:

it waits to be swelled by the movements
of flesh, bone and muscle; to have
life breathed into it. And yet,

all around the room white silk roses,
ungathered for the moment, are
springing from the furniture.

HIS AND HERS

Strange that wedding gifts should be so labelled.
Perhaps our cynical age has made us
believe in the certainty of divorce.

*No pre-nuptial contract? Mark everything
with name-tapes, ultra-violet pen; think of
the heartache that'll save, my dears, one day.*

These pink and blue monikers are, roughly,
as romantic as pissing up tree trunks
to prove that they stand in your territory.

Still, imagine the misty-focused joy
of stepping out of your shared bath-water
deliberately into the wrong towels.

COCOON

The day after the wedding
I wake in the bride's old bed,

champagne ghosts hammering at
the touchy cork of my head.

Kitchen. Coffee, family,
bacon, breathed-in cigarette,

and back upstairs to her room
to find, carefully laid, spread

across the duvet, her dress.
Linen, inhabited yet

by my sleep's warmth, seems to warm
her silk cocoon—shrugged and shed—

as if objects would keep her
here, as if she had upset

ghosts, as if life could be bred
from spores of perfume or sweat.

SUNDAY ORDINARINESS

'Though loving is hard, we want to say yes,
to be part of the Sunday ordinariness'—Robert Johnstone

Ordinary is a case of turning
a lazy eye on everyday magic.
Call me naive, but to say that any day

after this dawn-massive *yes* will be
ordinary is as shortsighted as
standing in fields, lost in brags of perfume

and the super-human architecture
of petal, stamen, sepal and leaf,
and pleading, *they're just flowers, only flowers.*

COCKATOO

The sulphur-crested cockatoo was bribed
with trinkets of cuttle-fish, regular
seed, to bear the clipping of its cramped wings,
the cold longitudes of its hemisphere;
for want of a rainforest, to make do
with central heating and aspidistra.

Red-eyed, stomping its fury on the perch,
this balding bird is all I remember
of the unknown couple. I was seven,
at most, when the man who had once poured out
every ounce of his unspeakable love
into details of my mother's dolls'-house

could not face a family in his home;
clocked more miles in his cab than usual.
We were hushed out like a secret, ten years
after my mother's room had been given
to tropical fish without memory
enough to rage against beguiling glass.

From the street I saw through the grey window
the cockatoo which my grandparents let,
in my memory, become them; pacing
the maddening doll-dimensions of home.
The uttermost end of my mother's line
carpeting its mean home with its own shit.

SECRET MARRIAGE

Two summers ago my sister returned
from a seaside trip with a photograph.
She and her boyfriend in false sepia,
stiff in formal Victorian costume;
dress, jacket and trousers as one-sided
as theatrical flats, but a neat trick.
The portrait had gathered a thin layer
of authenticating dust by this May,
when the fourteen hours' notice was given.

How marriage can break up the family
no one warns you. I know this second hand:
how my sister and her groom were cheered out
from the registry office garden to
a pony and carriage by the pavement—
a wedding car whose pollutions amount
to confetti and manure; food for birds
and new generations of bouquet blooms.

The charming anachronism passing
through slow traffic in the curious streets
must have seemed like a ghost of tradition
which the modern world can't quite lay to rest.
Trails of confetti falling on tarmac
made a path for the petrol-engine cars,
while the one mother present cried that this
is not how getting married used to be.

TOAST

Spitted on brass, floated over coals,
bread burns first around the crust—pale
squares with their dark frames of mundane
carcinogens;

like the black-edged envelopes which spoke
the *don't know how to say this* of
invitations to funerals
or the other.

LAST TRAIN HOME

for Norman MacCaig

Perhaps arriving is not a station
but the not-knowing if you are at rest
or infinite speed,

perhaps eternally the moment of
sun-blindness at the opening out
of a long tunnel.

OXFORD POETS

Fleur Adcock
Moniza Alvi
Joseph Brodsky
Basil Bunting
Tessa Rose Chester
Daniela Crăsnaru
Greg Delanty
Michael Donaghy
Keith Douglas
Antony Dunn
D. J. Enright
Roy Fisher
Ida Affleck Graves
Ivor Gurney
Gwen Harwood
Anthony Hecht
Zbigniew Herbert
Tobias Hill
Thomas Kinsella
Brad Leithauser
Jamie McKendrick

Sean O'Brien
Alice Oswald
Peter Porter
Craig Raine
Zsuzsa Rakovszky
Christopher Reid
Stephen Romer
Eva Salzman
Carole Satyamurti
Peter Scupham
Jo Shapcott
Penelope Shuttle
Goran Simić
Anne Stevenson
George Szirtes
Grete Tartler
Edward Thomas
Charles Tomlinson
Marina Tsvetaeva
Chris Wallace-Crabbe
Hugo Williams